Bobby Ch

Biography

Bobby Charlton: A Football Legend's Journey From Early Life, Career to Legacy; Dies at the Age of 86

Nora Ivey Press

Table of Contents

Introduction

On October 11, 1937, Bobby Charlton was born in Ashington, Northumberland, England. His family had a strong bond with the beautiful game when he was growing up. Three elder brothers played football, thus the love of the game ran in the family. His mother's cousin Jackie Milburn was a standout player for Newcastle United.

In 1953, Bobby, then barely eighteen years old, joined Manchester United's youth team, marking the beginning of an incredible adventure. The world had no idea that this youthful kid would grow up to be a timeless representation of football brilliance.

With his 1956 first-team debut, Bobby launched a career that would serve as an inspiration to countless players and fans. He quickly established himself as a regular part of the team and was a key member of the renowned "Busby Babes," a team of teenage athletes under the tutelage of the great Matt Busby. When they won the Football League First Division championship in 1957, their talent was evident.

But 1958 was the darkest period of Bobby's life. During a European Cup tournament, the team's aircraft met a tragic end in Munich, Germany. Although Bobby escaped the crash with great grace, the loss of eight teammates and three club employees had a lasting impact on his life.

Bobby bounced back from his injuries and kept wearing the Manchester United jersey despite the tragedy. He was instrumental in the team's accomplishments, winning the Football League championship in 1965 and 1967 in addition to the FA Cup in 1963. His skill on the pitch translated to the international arena, where he established himself as a vital member of the England national team, making 106 appearances and scoring 49 goals. His 1966 FIFA World Cup victory, in which he scored two goals in the historic final against West Germany at Wembley Stadium, was the apex of his international career. Among his many accomplishments, that year was winning the coveted Ballon d'Or for best player in Europe, and becoming the first English player to do so.

Although Bobby's victories abroad were impressive, his best season with the club came in 1968. He led Manchester United to its first-ever European Cup victory, making them the first English team to do it. Bobby's two goals in the 4-1 victory after extra time in the final versus Benfica at Wembley Stadium cemented his place in football history.

Bobby held both records when he left Manchester United in 1973, having played 758 appearances and scored 249 goals. He continued his football career by joining Preston North End as a player-manager, retiring from competition in 1975. But even after he made a brief comeback to the field in 1976—first for Waterford in Ireland and then for several Australian clubs—his passion for the game was still evident. In 1983, he even served as Wigan Athletic's interim manager for a brief period.

Bobby was married to Norma Ball in 1961, and the two had a long and happy marriage away from the field. The two girls of the couple were named Andrea and Suzanne. His close relationship with his brother Jack, a fellow football hero who departed in 2020, was indicative of the family's unwavering love for the game.

Bobby Charlton was a significant financial success; his estimated net worth was $25 million. His financial security came from his investments in businesses including restaurants, golf courses, and hotels. Bobby's altruism was evident even outside of his professional life as he contributed to several charities and causes, such as the Find A Better Way organization, the Bobby Charlton Soccer Schools, and the Laureus Sport for Good Foundation. His standing as a great gentleman and inspiration to others went well beyond the football field.

Bobby had a strong bond with football even after he stopped playing. He was one of Manchester United's directors from 1984 until he died in 2023. In addition, he served as a member of FIFA's Football Committee and vice-president of the Football

Association. In 1994, Queen Elizabeth II awarded Bobby a knighthood in recognition of his achievements; throughout his life, he also won various other honors and distinctions.

Bobby Charlton's adventure came to an emotional end on October 21, 2023. Despite fighting dementia for several years, his legacy lived on. Millions of fans and players around the world grieved over his passing, remembering him as one of the greatest football players of all time and a real gentleman. His impact on both society and sport is still felt today.

This book chronicles Bobby Charlton's incredible journey from his upbringing and early years to his illustrious career and post-football life. It also explores his private life, achievements in business, health issues, and the announcement of his death. It is an homage to a legendary football player whose skill, passion, leadership, and character inspired countless players and fans throughout the years.

Chapter One:Early Life and Background

The narrative of Bobby Charlton starts in the sleepy English town of Ashington, Northumberland. October 11, 1937, a date that would go down in football history, was when he was born. Though it was remote from the busy stadiums and boisterous spectators, this northern village was the birthplace of a legend.

Football was deeply ingrained in Ashington's community. Bobby Charlton was just another child from that kind of place who dreamed of being a football hero. However, he had a stronger bond with the beautiful game than most. You see, the Charlton family enjoyed playing football together.

Jackie Milburn was Bobby's mother's cousin—a name that strikes a chord in Newcastle United fans' hearts like a symphony. Jackie Milburn was a star, an inspiration, and a living legend in addition to being a football player. His achievements on the field created a long shadow, which also covered young Bobby.

Bobby was raised in a football-loving family and was exposed to the sport's legends, victories, and sometimes heartbreaks. He had three older siblings who were all accomplished football players. You could say that football skill was raised in the Charlton family.

The beautiful game was a common topic of conversation in the living room, with stories of goals, matches, and special moments. Bobby took in every bit of the passionately charged environment. He heard tales of triumph and tragedy, the exhilaration of winning and the anguish of losing. These tales were more than just anecdotes; they contained lessons that Bobby would apply to his professional life.

He spent his early years attending school and hanging out with pals to play football in the streets. When Bobby booted a ball, there was an obvious glitter in his eyes. It was his vocation, his destiny, and more than simply a hobby.

At the youthful age of sixteen, Bobby took a big step toward his football aspirations in 1953. He joined Manchester United's youth team, one of the most well-known football teams in England. For the young man from Ashington, it was a historic opportunity to leave the safety of a small town and enter the big stage.

Talent, drive, and a passionate interest in the sport were the cornerstones of the path to fame. Bobby had no idea that he would soon be a part of a legendary chapter in football history, but his adventure had begun.

This marked the start of an incredible journey in which a young man from a small English village who loved football would go on to become a worldwide symbol of the beautiful game. Bobby Charlton's life narrative was just getting started, but it would be filled with passion and commitment that would make a lasting impression on the football community.

Join us as we explore Bobby Charlton's life narrative, which includes both triumph and sorrow, iconic on-field experiences, and lasting contributions to the sport. Here is where the Bobby Charlton tale begins, and you are cordially encouraged to take part.

Chapter Two:Rise to Stardom

Bobby Charlton's initial steps into the professional football scene were shown to us in the previous chapter when he joined Manchester United's youth team. We'll now go into more detail about his journey as we continue to explore how he became well-known and influential in the football community.

Bobby's career took a significant turn when he moved from the youth squad to the main team. In 1956, at the tender age of 18, he demonstrated a youthful aptitude and tenacity that belied his years. Making the transition from the junior team to the senior squad was an incredible accomplishment, and Bobby was going to show that he was one of the best.

There was excitement in the air as he entered the pitch donning the recognizable red and white Manchester United jersey. This was the beginning of something exceptional, not only for Bobby but also for the entire football community. He was well-prepared for the trials that lay ahead thanks to his youth.

These young, gifted players were known as the 'Busby Babes,' and they were coached by their esteemed manager, Sir Matt Busby. Among these burgeoning talents was Bobby Charlton, and the two of them set out on a trip that would go down in history.

This young team accomplished something in 1957 that many believed to be beyond their years. Their incredible achievement of winning the Football League First Division title cemented their legacy in football history. The image of Bobby Charlton directing plays and displaying his abilities on the pitch inspired sports enthusiasts throughout the nation.

There was an obvious sense of togetherness among the players, and their bond went beyond the game. They had a dream that brought them together to become more than simply teammates—they were like family. Bobby Charlton was central to the 'Busby Babes' movement, which represented the future of English football.

But occasionally, the stormiest skies are also home to the brightest stars. With a power that would alter Bobby's life forever, catastrophe struck in 1958. The 'Busby Babes' were returning from a European Cup play when Munich, Germany, saw a tragic event.

The team's aspirations and dreams were dashed when the plane transporting them crashed. On that awful day, three members of the club staff and eight of Bobby's teammates perished. Bobby lived through the ordeal, but for the rest of his life, he was physically and psychologically scarred.

In this heartbreaking phase of Bobby Charlton's life, the crushing weight of loss was paired with the highs of triumph. It shows evidence of the tenacity and resolve that would characterize his professional life. The 'Busby Babes' weren't broken; they were just scared. Out of tragedy, Bobby Charlton in particular would rise to become one of the greatest football legends in history.

We'll look at Bobby's recovery from the horrific Munich Air Disaster and how he went on to play for Manchester United, contributing to their further success, in the upcoming chapter. Once again, his unwavering brilliance and energy would be evident as he served as an inspiration and ray of hope for both a grieving squad and a country.

Chapter Three: Triumph and Tragedy

We covered Bobby Charlton's life story and family history in the earlier chapters, as well as his ascent to fame with the "Busby Babes." We are about to embark on a chapter of success and tragedy that will put Bobby's fortitude and character to the ultimate test.

Bobby was about to embark on a bright future with Manchester United in 1958. With youthful players like Bobby at the core of their success, the team was rejoicing in the aftermath of winning the Football League First Division title.

But in football, as in life, exuberance may give way to unbearable sadness very quickly. The 'Busby Babes' set off on a voyage that would forever change Bobby Charlton's life and the entire footballing world on that fateful day, February 6, 1958.

With great expectations, the team was returning from a European Cup encounter. But disaster happened as the aircraft carrying them tried to take off from Munich-Riem Airport's slush-covered runway. Heartbreak and misery trailed behind the aircraft when it crashed.

Three devoted club employees and eight of Bobby's best friends were killed in the wreckage. These young guys, full of promise for a brilliant future and having already accomplished so much, had their goals and aspirations dashed in the blink of an eye. The world and the football community both lamented this immense loss.

Bobby Charlton himself was remarkably spared from the collision, but he was emotionally and physically severely damaged when he came to. A weaker man might have been broken by the injuries he received, but Bobby was unbroken. Even at his lowest points, his unwavering determination to overcome hardship and his unbreakable spirit were evident.

Bobby's life changed dramatically as a result of this heartbreaking chapter. It was evidence of his tenacity and inner might. It served as a sobering reminder of both the transience of life and the resilience of the human spirit.

As we follow Bobby Charlton's life, we will see how, in addition to being a football player, he rose from the ashes of that tragic day to become an inspiration and source of hope. The tale of Bobby Charlton is one of overcoming hardship, and it is a tale that will enthrall and motivate future generations.

Chapter Four:Legendary Career

The tale of Bobby Charlton is one of tenacity and unrelenting resolve. We discussed Bobby's survival and the awful circumstances of the Munich Air Disaster in the last chapter. We now carry on with our exploration of Bobby Charlton's illustrious career, which helped to establish him as one of the greatest football players of all time.

Despite his physical and psychological wounds from the Munich Air Disaster, Bobby refused to let the catastrophe define him. Rather, he turned it into motivation to intensify his love for the game. He made a comeback to the Manchester United field, inspiring and motivating not only his teammates but also football fans everywhere.

The years that ensued bore witness to his tremendous talent and unwavering resolve. Bobby developed as a crucial component of Manchester United's comeback. It was obvious that his best playing days were yet ahead of him as he was instrumental in the team's 1963 FA Cup victory.

Bobby's accomplishments, though, went beyond the club scene. With the England national team, he kept shining on the international scene. He made his national team debut in 1958, and he became an important member very soon after. In his international career, the 1966 FIFA World Cup in England was a turning point.

Bobby Charlton's genius was evident in the final at Wembley Stadium versus West Germany. With two vital goals, he helped England win their first and only World Cup. America exulted, and Bobby rose to prominence as a genuine national hero. His ability to score goals, vision, and technique was astounding, and they won him the coveted Ballon d'Or trophy that year, making him the first player from England to do so.

Bobby Charlton was a complete midfield player who was renowned for his outstanding passing, inventiveness, and work ethic. He was not merely a talented attacker. He excels beyond his contemporaries due to his ability to control the midfield and create cutting passes. His knowledge of the game was unparalleled, and his football acumen was unmatched.

Manchester United enjoyed further success as his career there flourished, winning the Football League titles in 1965 and 1967. During this time, Bobby Charlton cemented his status as one of the greatest football players in history. His playing style was appreciated by fans all around the world, and his name was synonymous with genius.

Still, his greatest club accomplishment remained to come. Bobby led Manchester United to the European Cup win in 1968, an achievement that went beyond club football. Bobby was instrumental in the thrilling match between his team and Benfica at Wembley Stadium, helping them win 4-1 after extra time with two goals from him. Manchester United were the first English club to win the European Cup, making it a historic occasion.

Bobby's great career was highlighted by a plethora of memorable events, such as incredible goals, astute assists, and outstanding leadership both on and off the field. His legacy will always be with Manchester United, and the club's achievements have come to be associated with him.

Bobby's lasting impact and contribution to the game would go well beyond his playing career. We'll look at how Bobby shaped the football world in the upcoming chapters, both as a coach and in other administrative capacities, leaving a lasting legacy that inspires and influences the beautiful game.

Chapter Five:Life Beyond Football

The journey of Bobby Charlton has taken us from his early years to his World Cup victory and club successes—the highs and lows of his illustrious football career. We are now moving on to the following chapter, which delves into Bobby's life off the football field, his responsibilities as a coach, and his ventures into several administrative posts.

As Bobby's playing career developed, he started to think about what he would do when he retired from competitive play. During this period of change, he tried to pass on his extensive understanding of the game to the upcoming football players.

Bobby's first coaching role occurred in 1973 when he joined Preston North End as a player-manager. In this capacity, he was able to pass on his enthusiasm for football to younger players by sharing his knowledge and insight.

Bobby led by example off the field as well, demonstrating his leadership abilities and commitment to the game. He had a talent for deciphering the subtleties of the game and inspiring his team to perform to the best of their abilities.

He decided to give up playing in 1975, bringing an incredible on-field career to an end. Even though his playing days were ended, he remained very much involved with football. He made a lasting impression on the football community while serving as an ambassador for the game.

However, Bobby found it difficult to ignore the pull of the game. He made a brief comeback to the field for Waterford in Ireland in 1976, proving that his love for the game would never die. He demonstrated glimmers of the genius that had made him a household name even at this point in his career.

Bobby's football career extended beyond the borders of England and Ireland. He kept pushing himself, playing for Australian teams including Perth Azzurri, Newcastle KB United, and Blacktown City. A new generation of football players in Australia was inspired by him in addition to drawing large audiences when he was on these teams.

In addition to his playing career, Bobby also dabbled in coaching, joining Wigan Athletic as a temporary manager in 1983. He was able to share his expertise and love of the game differently through his work as a manager and coach.

Bobby Charlton made significant contributions to football both as a player and coach, but his influence went beyond the field. He had an unrelenting devotion to the game and utilized his power to influence how football would develop in the future.

The various phases of Bobby's life bear witness to the sport's enduring force as well as the influence of a single man's enthusiasm and dedication. We will delve further into his connections, personal life, and struggles as we follow his path. The life story of Bobby Charlton is not just about football; it's also a monument to the resilience of a legend who had a lasting impression on both the game and society at large.

Chapter Six:Personal Life

We have traveled through Bobby Charlton's early years, as well as his ascent to football fame and his accomplishments as a player and coach. This time, we get further into the football legend's personal life, learning about his relationships, family, and struggles.

In Bobby's personal life, relationships and the bonds he forged with his loved ones were more important than football. He married Norma Ball in 1961, marking the start of a new chapter in his life. A long and joyful marriage that would continue for decades began with this union.

Bobby's wife Norma supported him both professionally and personally, acting as more than just a companion. Their enduring love story served as a monument to the strength of love and devotion. Bobby found stability and comfort in their partnership, which withstood the ups and downs of the football world.

The center of the couple's family life were their two children, Suzanne and Andrea. For Bobby, his function as a father held equal significance to that of his position on the football field. He was a devoted family man who enjoyed being with his loved ones and making priceless memories that would last a lifetime.

Bobby always understood the value of family, even in the face of his popularity and prosperity. He didn't lose perspective, appreciating his wife and kids' love and support. This period of his life served as a reminder that, despite their fame, football legends are just regular individuals with incredible tales to tell.

But Bobby had problems in his personal life, just like the rest of us. These were not only football-related difficulties. We shall examine Bobby's finances, net worth, and the range of entrepreneurial endeavors he undertook beyond athletics in the upcoming chapter. It is evidence of his broad interests and the willpower that propelled him to achieve success in all spheres of his life.

Chapter Seven:Net Worth

This chapter delves into Bobby Charlton's financial life, examining his investments, net worth, and commercial endeavors. Bobby's football career brought him recognition and fortune, but his varied hobbies and sound financial management contributed much to the shape of his post-football life.

Bobby Charlton's estimated net worth of $25 million is a result of his prosperous football career and his subsequent engagement in several business endeavors. Bobby showed himself to be an astute investor and businessman outside of the pitch.

Owning hotels, restaurants, and golf courses was one of his noteworthy investments. Through these endeavors, he was able to broaden his sources of income and discover new opportunities outside of sports. His goals for success went beyond the pitch, and he intended to leave an impact on the business community as well.

His tenacity and foresight were demonstrated by his business drive and the monetary gains that followed. Bobby's commercial achievements proved that he was more than simply a football legend; in addition, he was a cunning businessman who saw the need to make wise investments.

Bobby Charlton's major source of fame and first love was football, but his financial success also enabled him to promote causes close to his heart and ensure his family's future. It demonstrated his dedication to excellence on and off the field.

We will go into a different aspect of Bobby's life in the upcoming chapter, including his health issues and the announcement of his death. This chapter serves as a moving reminder that nobody is exempt from life's hardships—not even legendary people. Bobby's story is not only one of success; it also demonstrates his fortitude in the face of difficulty.

Chapter Eight: Health Challenge and News of Death

This chapter brings us to a depressing point in Bobby Charlton's life as we examine the health issues he dealt with in his latter years and the announcement of his death. This chapter serves as a helpful reminder that everyone is susceptible to life's imperfections, including legends.

Dementia became Bobby's formidable enemy as he grew older. This crippling illness presented him and his family with many difficulties. Even for someone as strong and tough as

Bobby, it served as a sobering reminder of how fleeting life is.

Bobby's supporters and the footballing community were deeply moved by the revelation of his fight with dementia. His health battle was revealed to the world at a dramatic moment that underscored the significance of increasing awareness of this illness. Bobby's strength of character was demonstrated by his bravery in facing dementia and the assistance he received from his loved ones.

The world was devastated to learn of Bobby Charlton's death at the age of 86 on October 21, 2023. His passing signaled the end of an era and created an enduring loss in the football community. Millions of fans and players observed a minute of sadness, recalling him as a wonderful gentleman in addition to being one of the greatest football players of all time. Bobby has left a lasting and indisputable legacy in both sports and society. He never stopped inspiring in his later years, not just with his prior accomplishments but also with his ability to bounce back from hardship. His trip served as a monument to the resilience of the human spirit, and he will always be remembered as a legendary football player.

We consider Bobby Charlton's influence on the football world and the hearts of his admirers as we wrap up this chapter. Generations to come will find inspiration in his story, which is a monument to the enduring force of passion, dedication, and character.

Chapter Nine:Legacy and Influence

In this last part, we consider Bobby Charlton's enduring legacy and his significant impact on the football community and beyond. His is a story of a life that inspires and influences generations in addition to a spectacular football career.

There is no denying Bobby Charlton's influence in the football world. He was not merely a talented athlete; he represented greatness and sportsmanship. His achievements with the England national team, his tenure at Manchester United, and his accolades cemented his status as one of the greatest football players of all time.

His leadership instilled a lasting legacy in the sport, both on and off the field. He was more than just a captain; he set an exemplary example for others to follow. He was well-liked by both players and fans for his modesty, work ethic, and devotion to the game. He was the epitome of everything football stands for—a true gentleman of the game.

Bobby had a huge impact on the football field as well. His efforts to improve the world were demonstrated by his humanitarian causes, which included his support of the Bobby Charlton Soccer Schools, the Laureus Sport for Good Foundation, and the

Find A Better Way organization. He left behind a legacy of kindness and compassion by using his success and notoriety to support causes that were important to him.

In 1994, Queen Elizabeth II knighted Bobby in honor of his achievements in the game. Throughout his life, he was bestowed with several honors and distinctions that spoke to the great regard and appreciation he was shown by people worldwide.

Beyond his accomplishments, Bobby's influence as an administrator helped to shape the football environment. From 1984 until his death, he was a director of Manchester United, overseeing the growth and success of the team. To further solidify his position in the administration of the sport, he served as a member of FIFA's Football Committee and vice-president of the Football Association.

Bobby Charlton's narrative is about more than simply football; it's about the lasting influence of character, passion, and hard work. He was a gentleman, a football star, and a humanitarian who made use of his power for the benefit of society. His legacy endures, motivating upcoming generations to strive for excellence on and off the field.

We honor the enduring legacy of an honor great whose life continues to inspire and influence the sport and society as we wrap up this chapter and Bobby's incredible narrative. Bobby

Charlton is a legend who had an enduring impression on the game and will always be remembered.

Conclusion

In conclusion, Bobby Charlton's life and career serve as a tribute to the enduring strength of character, passion, and determination. Bobby's narrative is one of perseverance in the face of hardship, from his modest upbringing in Ashington, Northumberland, to the sacred grounds of Old Trafford and Wembley Stadium. His legacy is one of inspiration.

Bobby Charlton was a symbol of excellence and sportsmanship in addition to being a talented football player. One of the greatest football players of all time, he achieved success with the England national team and had a successful career with Manchester United. He was hailed as a real gentleman of the game for his leadership, both on and off the field, which made a lasting impression on the sport.

Bobby's humanitarian activities demonstrated his dedication to changing the world for the better outside of football. He left behind a legacy of kindness and compassion by using his success and notoriety to support causes that were important to him.

Bobby was a key administrator who helped to shape the football world. His commitment to the management and advancement of sport was evident through his work with FIFA, the

Football Association, and Manchester United.

Bobby experienced health issues in his final years, including dementia. His fortitude in the face of hardship served as an example, highlighting the significance of bringing attention to these circumstances.

The world mourned the loss of a football legend on October 21, 2023. Bobby Charlton's legacy endures, motivating upcoming generations to strive for excellence on and off the field.

His narrative serves as a reminder that even football legends face hardships in life and is not only about football. The life of Bobby Charlton is evidence of the resilience of a legend who had a profound impact on both the globe and sports. Future generations will be impacted by his legacy in both society and the great game.

Printed in Great Britain
by Amazon

33726818R00036